A Nation Divided
Causes of the Civil War

Jeff Putnam

CRABTREE
Publishing Company
www.crabtreebooks.com

Author: Jeff Putnam
Publishing plan research and development:
  Sean Charlebois, Reagan Miller
  Crabtree Publishing Company
Editors: Mark Cheatham, Kirsten Holm, Lynn Peppas
Proofreader: Wendy Scavuzzo
Editorial director: Kathy Middleton
Production coordinator: Shivi Sharma
Creative director: Arka Roy Chaudhary
Design: Sandy Kent
Cover design: Samara Parent
Photo research: Iti Shrotriya
Maps: Paul Brinkdopke
Production coordinator: Margaret Amy Salter
Prepress technician: Margaret Amy Salter
Print coordinator: Katherine Berti

Written, developed, and produced by Planman Technologies

Front cover (top) and back cover (background): A military map of the United States from 1862 showing forts and military posts.
Front cover (bottom): A political cartoon showing General George McClellan attempting to mediate between President Abraham Lincoln and Jefferson Davis.
Back cover (logo): A civil war era cannon stands in front of the flag from Fort Sumter.

Photographs and Reproductions
Front cover (top) and back cover (background): Wikimedia Commons: Johnson, A. J.; Front cover (bottom): Library of Congress: Currier & Ives; Title Page (p. 1): THE BRIDGEMAN ART LIBRARY/Photolibrary (top), Bettmann/CORBIS/Click Photos; Table of Contents (p. 3): Chapter 1: North Wind / North Wind Picture Archives, Chapters 2-6: Library of Congress; Chapter Opener image (pp. 5, 11, 21, 29, 35, 39): North Wind / North Wind Picture Archives Bettmann/CORBIS/Click Photos: p. 23 (bottom); THE BRIDGEMAN ART LIBRARY/Photolibrary: p. 10 (bottom), 18; The Granger Collection, New York: p. 34; Library of Congress: pp. 4, 10 (top), 12, 15, 16, 22, 23 (top), 24 (top and bottom), 25, 26, 27, 28, 30, 31, 36 (top, center, bottom), 37, 41, 43; North Wind / North Wind Picture Archives: pp. 6, 7, 8, 9, 14, 19

Title page (top): Southern cotton was transported by steamship to ports such as New Orleans, then put on ocean-going ships for transport to Northern cities and Britain.
Title page (bottom): Boston citizens protest an 1854 court order to return Anthony Burns to slavery in Virginia.

Library and Archives Canada Cataloguing in Publication

Putnam, Jeff, 1951-
    A nation divided : causes of the Civil War / Jeff Putnam.

(Understanding the Civil War)
Includes index.
Issued also in electronic formats.
ISBN 978-0-7787-5337-7 (bound).--ISBN 978-0-7787-5354-4 (pbk.)

    1. United States--History--Civil War, 1861-1865--Causes--Juvenile literature. 2. United States--Politics and government--1849-1861--Juvenile literature. I. Title. II. Series: Understanding the Civil War

E459.P88 2011   j973.7'11   C2011-907480-X

Library of Congress Cataloging-in-Publication Data

Putnam, Jeff.
    A Nation divided : causes of the Civil War / Jeff Putnam.
    p. cm. -- (Understanding the Civil War)
    Includes index.
    ISBN 978-0-7787-5337-7 (reinforced library binding : alk. paper) -- ISBN 978-0-7787-5354-4 (pbk. : alk. paper) -- ISBN 978-1-4271-9936-2 (electronic pdf.) -- ISBN 978-1-4271-9945-4 (electronic html.)
    1. United States--History--Civil War, 1861-1865--Causes--Juvenile literature. I. Title.

E459.P94 2011
973.7'11--dc23
                                                            2011045080

Crabtree Publishing Company
www.crabtreebooks.com   1-800-387-7650

Printed in the U.S.A./122016/CG20161021

Copyright © 2012 CRABTREE PUBLISHING COMPANY. All rights reserved. No part of this publication may be reproduced, stored in a retrieval system or be transmitted in any form or by any means, electronic, mechanical, photocopying, recording, or otherwise, without the prior written permission of Crabtree Publishing Company.

Published in Canada
Crabtree Publishing
616 Welland Ave.
St. Catharines, Ontario
L2M 5V6

Published in the United States
Crabtree Publishing
PMB 59051
350 Fifth Avenue, 59th Floor
New York, New York 10118

Published in the United Kingdom
Crabtree Publishing
Maritime House
Basin Road North, Hove
BN41 1WR

Published in Australia
Crabtree Publishing
3 Charles Street
Coburg North
VIC 3058

TABLE of CONTENTS

1 — *A Nation Torn Apart* — 5
One Election, Many Candidates | A New Nation
Winds of Change | The Beginnings of Sectionalism

2 — *Social and Cultural Divisions: North and South* — 11
Defining North and South | The Search for Compromise
Two Regions | The North | The South

3 — *Divided on Slavery* — 21
Slaves in the United States | Slavery and Laws
Slavery and Popular Culture
Rising Tensions Over Slavery

4 — *Political Divisions* — 29
Political Parties Disagree About Slavery | National
Political Parties | Western Expansion Raises Tensions
Congress Addresses Slavery

5 — *The Election of 1860* — 35
The Nominating Conventions | The Campaign of 1860
Counting the Votes

6 — *The Union Broken* — 39
Why Did States Secede? | The Road to War

Glossary, 45 | More Information, 47 | Index, 48

> *In your hands, my dissatisfied fellow countrymen, and not in mine, is the momentous issue of civil war. The government will not assail you. You can have no conflict, without being yourselves the aggressors. You have no oath registered in Heaven to destroy the government, while I shall have the most solemn one to 'preserve, protect and defend' it.*
> —President Abraham Lincoln's First Inaugural Address, March 4, 1861

The U.S. Capitol during President Abraham Lincoln's first inauguration, March 4, 1861

A Nation Torn Apart

Almost every American was sure of one thing in the fall of 1860. The upcoming presidential election would be a turning point for the nation. Many were unsure of how they had arrived at this point and what the future held.

One Election, Many Candidates

The candidate of the newly formed Republican Party was Abraham Lincoln. Many Americans considered him to be against slavery. The Democratic Party was bitterly divided over the slavery issue. Northern Democrats chose Stephen Douglas. He believed states should be free to make their own decisions about slavery. Southern Democrats were angry that Douglas would not **endorse** slavery. They supported Vice-President John C. Breckinridge. A fourth candidate, John Bell, gained the nomination of the Constitutional Union Party. This party took no position on slavery. It claimed only to stand for "the Constitution . . . the Union . . . and the Enforcement of the Laws."

Lincoln won the election. Although disagreements between the North and South had been smoldering for many years, his victory became the spark that ignited the Civil War.

Major Events

1787 U.S. Constitution written

1803 Louisiana Purchase

1808 Slave trade outlawed

1825 Erie Canal completed

1833 American Anti-Slavery Society founded

> *In your hands . . . my fellow countrymen . . . is the issue of civil war. . . . You can have no conflict without being yourselves the aggressors.*
> —President Abraham Lincoln's first inaugural address, March 4, 1861

A Nation Divided: Causes of the Civil War

A New Nation

In the year 1800, the United States was barely 25 years old. The Constitution had been written only 13 years before. It created a system of government in the United States. The country's population was small, a little more than five million. There were few large cities. Most people lived on farms or in villages and small towns. Some settlers had crossed the Appalachian Mountains, but most Americans still lived near the east coast.

Who Were Americans?

At the end of the 1700s, most Americans from the North and South shared many beliefs and values. Most were Protestants. A few were Catholics and Jews. Most were Northern Europeans, except for Africans and Native Americans. Few Americans traveled far from where they were born. Farmers grew food for their families and neighbors. Local craftspeople made most items people needed. There were only a handful of industries.

In the early 1800s, most Americans lived on farms or in small towns.

What Did Americans Believe?

Many Americans feared a strong central, or **federal**, government that had more power than individual states. They believed states could best decide how their economies should be formed and run. They also thought a strong central government might limit individual rights. This view was common in the South and in the frontier regions of the Midwest. On the other hand, some people, especially Northern businessmen, supported a strong central government. They hoped a central government could use its power to shape economic development. For example, it could pass laws to support manufacturing and trade or encourage the building of roads, canals, and railroads.

Americans in the North and the Upper Midwest generally opposed slavery. Americans in the South and Southwest supported it.

A Nation Torn Apart

Winds of Change

Big changes were occurring in the United States around 1825. Population growth, immigration, geographic expansion, and the development of **industry** played major roles in these changes. Hundreds of thousands of Europeans, mostly British and Irish, were moving to the United States every year. Much of the eastern coast was already settled. Therefore, large numbers of new citizens were moving west to settle new, untamed areas of land.

The industrial age that began in Great Britain was beginning to take root in Northern states. Wherever they lived, though, Americans were hopeful about the future. They felt their country would soon take its place among the great nations of the world.

> *They say I'm now in freedom's land,*
> *Where all men masters be;*
> *But were I in my winding-sheet*,*
> *There's none to care for me.*
>
> —Irish immigration song
> *sheet for wrapping a dead body

More People

In the first half of the 1800s, five million immigrants arrived, most of them from Europe. Another factor that led to an increase in population was how people lived. In general, Americans were healthy people. They lived longer than people in Europe. They ate more and better food and had more children. They got sick less often because most of them were not packed into filthy cities. All of these factors helped the population rise. It grew from 5 million to 32 million in the years between 1800 to 1860.

Where Americans lived and worked also began to change. The **urban** population grew three times faster than the **rural** population. Americans were leaving their farms to live and work in cities. By 1860, about 50 percent of Americans worked on farms.

European immigrants leaving for America

7

A Nation Divided: Causes of the Civil War

Westward Ho!

In 1800, the map of the United States looked very much like it did at the time of the American Revolution. Almost all Americans lived east of these Appalachian Mountains. Only two states west of the mountains, Kentucky and Tennessee, had joined the Union.

In 1803, however, President Thomas Jefferson doubled the size of the country. He bought the Louisiana Territory from France. By the end of the 1840s, the country stretched from the Atlantic Ocean to the Pacific Ocean. The territories of Texas, Florida, Oregon, and California were added. Americans streamed west into these new lands.

The Rise of Industry

Improved transportation following the War of 1812 spurred the development of industry. Before the war, almost all manufactured goods came from Britain because it was easier and cheaper to import goods from across the Atlantic Ocean. The building of roads and canals made it possible to ship goods more cheaply within the country. The most important transportation advance was the railroads. By 1860, the United States had more miles (km) of track than the rest of the world combined.

Factories were built along transportation lines such as rivers or railroads. They made products such as cloth, shoes, machinery, furniture, and tools. These factories employed men, women, and children. They helped give the United States the world's highest **standard of living**. The United States also had the world's second-highest **industrial output**.

What Do You Know!

THE LOUISIANA PURCHASE

In 1802, President Thomas Jefferson sent an ambassador to France to make an offer to buy the port city of New Orleans. This would ensure that American farmers could continue to sell their goods to Europe. The French offered to sell all of the Louisiana Territory. Jefferson accepted and Congress approved the purchase in 1803 for $15 million. The Louisiana Purchase roughly doubled the size of the United States.

> *Oh! isn't it a pity, such a pretty girl as I, Should be sent to the factory to pine away and die?*
>
> —protest song popular with textile factory girls in Lowell, Massachusetts

Railroads were an important means of transporting goods and people. At left is a timetable for the Albany & Buffalo line in 1843.

The Beginnings of Sectionalism

People began to identify more with their region than with others across the country. **Sectionalism**, or identifying strongly with one's region, began to take hold. Experiences with immigration, westward expansion, and industrialization were different from one region to the next. Different parts of the country were developing at different rates and in different ways.

The North: A New Way of Thinking

Most of the industries in the United States were located in the North. The area was rich in natural resources needed to power them. There were businessmen willing to use their money to develop the industries.

Many skilled European laborers came to the area in search of work. Most settled in the Northeast or Midwest in the newly purchased area of land from the Louisiana Purchase. Many immigrants brought with them their ways of life and beliefs, such as the Catholic religion.

The South: Farming and Slavery

There was a different way of life in the South. It was still overwhelmingly agricultural. Its main products—cotton, rice, and sugar—were produced mostly using slave labor. The South lagged behind the North in miles (km) of railroads, population growth, industry, and other economic measures.

The differences between the North and South helped create a feeling of sectionalism. People began to think of themselves as Northerners and Southerners because of these differences. They believed they had different values and different economic interests.

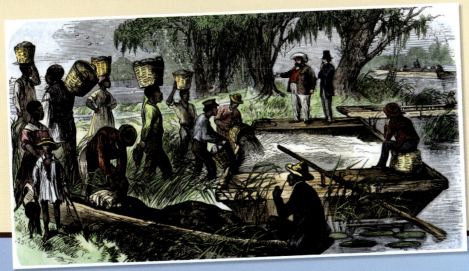

Slaves loading rice from a plantation onto a barge in the Savannah River, Georgia

A Nation Divided: Causes of the Civil War

Right: An abolitionist print depicting the slave trade. Africans, bound in chains, are being sold by the man on horseback. The dome of the U.S. Capitol appears in the distance.

An advertisement for slaves to be sold at auction

Fanning the Flames

Events also helped create this feeling of difference. The importation of new African slaves had been banned in 1808, but slavery was legal in many states. New states entering the Union between 1820 and 1850 faced the problem of allowing or banning slavery. Those against slavery believed it should not be allowed in new states. Supporters of slavery felt settlers from the South should be able to bring their way of life with them. These opposing views of slavery caused tensions between North and South.

A political crisis flared up in 1832. Some Southerners claimed states had the right to **nullify**, or refuse to obey, federal laws. Most Northerners, and President Andrew Jackson of Tennessee, disagreed.

The growth of **abolitionist** societies in the North also increased tensions between North and South. Abolitionists wanted to put an end to slavery.

Cautious Optimism

In spite of rising tensions, few Americans expected sectional differences to lead to war. People looked back at the compromises that brought the new nation together under the Constitution. They believed the country would find a way out of its difficulties, just as it had earlier.

Social and Cultural Divisions: North and South

Americans were similar in many ways. They shared an inspiring history. They felt pride in their young country. Most practiced the same religion. Even though there were similarities, there were many differences, too. People from the North or South regions were growing further apart. The economies of their regions were different. Their ideas of government clashed. Each region had different hopes for the future.

The North and South also held strong views about each other. These strong views threatened to cause a **sectional crisis**, or disagreement between sections of a country. Many feared a sectional crisis could destroy the unity of the country.

Major Events

1763 — Mason-Dixon Line begun

1787 — Northwest Territory acquired

1803 — Louisiana Territory purchased

1820 — Missouri Compromise

Defining North and South

Two Englishmen, an astronomer named Charles Mason and a surveyor named Jeremiah Dixon, are known today for a line that bears their names. They were asked in 1763 to settle a longstanding argument between two important families. The Penn family had founded the colony of Pennsylvania. The Calvert family founded Maryland. The two families disagreed on the boundary between the two colonies. It took the men five years to lay out the Mason-Dixon

Line. They marked the 233-mile (375 km) Pennsylvania-Maryland boundary with huge blocks of limestone. For another 83 miles (134 km), the line separated Maryland and Delaware.

Charles Mason and Jeremiah Dixon had traveled the world studying eclipses, comets, and other sky events. They used their knowledge of the stars and astronomical instruments to determine state boundaries. Attacks by Indians prevented them from completing the last 36 miles (58 km) of the line.

The Mason-Dixon Line did more than separate states. In the minds of most Americans at the time, it divided the North from the South. It divided two cultures and two ways of viewing society.

The Search for Compromise

The question of slavery had troubled the country from its very beginning. The men who wrote the Constitution were unable to find a satisfactory answer. They passed the problem on to future generations of Americans. One of the first attempts to deal with slavery was the Missouri Compromise of 1820.

This illustration shows slaves using an early cotton gin to separate cotton fibers from seeds. This invention brought about huge growth in cotton production in the South, and slave ownership grew dramatically.

Growth Leads to Conflict

The first large addition of land to the United States was the Northwest Territory in 1787. This was the area north of the Ohio River and east of the Mississippi River. Congress decided there would be no slavery in states formed from this area.

Just a few years later, in 1803, the United States purchased the vast Louisiana Territory. Immediately, people from the east began to move west. As they moved, they took their ideas with them. Settlers from the South expected to take enslaved people.

Social and Cultural Divisions: North and South

The Missouri Compromise

By 1820, the United States government knew it had to do something to address slavery in the territories. Its answer was a compromise. A **compromise** is an agreement in which each side gets just part of what it wants. Congress said there would be no slavery north of the latitude line 36°30´N. This is the line that today forms most of the border between Arkansas and Missouri.

The compromise was mostly the work of Henry Clay, an influential senator from Kentucky. It made an exception for the new state of Missouri. Missourians would be allowed to own slaves. Maine, which broke away from Massachusetts, became a state at the same time. Maine would enter the Union as a free state.

By accepting two new states at the same time, one free and one not, the compromise maintained the delicate balance between free and slave states. For 30 years, the Missouri Compromise solved this difficult problem, but it was not a final solution.

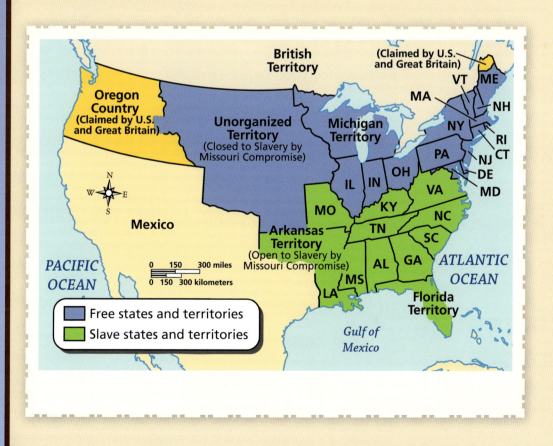

A Nation Divided: Causes of the Civil War

Two Regions

At the time of the Missouri Compromise, the North included New England, New York, Pennsylvania, and New Jersey. Further west, Ohio, Indiana, and Illinois were free states. The South consisted of Virginia, North Carolina, South Carolina, Georgia, Alabama, Mississippi, Tennessee, and Louisiana. Several states that had not banned slavery were considered border states: Missouri, Delaware, Maryland, and Kentucky.

The North

By almost all measurements, the North was growing more powerful economically through the early 1800s. Its population was larger, and it had more big cities. It had more factories, railroads, and canals. It had better communications, such as the telegraph, invented in 1844. Northern farmers usually owned their own land.

Cities and Immigration

Northern cities built more factories. People moved to Northern cities in search of work. Job seekers included native-born Americans as well as skilled, immigrant laborers from Europe. Small towns and villages, such as Buffalo, Pittsburgh, Cincinnati, Chicago, and St. Louis, quickly grew into important cities.

Cotton mills in Lowell, Massachusetts. Northern cotton mills used Southern cotton grown using slave labor.

Immigration to the United States grew dramatically, beginning around 1840. The largest groups came from Ireland and Germany. Many settled in big cities such as New York, Philadelphia, Boston, and Chicago. Immigrants brought their religions, languages, and cultures with them. These new ways of life caused tensions with native-born Americans.

Social and Cultural Divisions: North and South

Religion in the North

Most Northerners were Protestants. Many shared similar values. They believed in thriftiness, or using money carefully. They were not afraid of hard work. There were Catholics and other religious groups in the North also. People who shared Protestant values, however, became the leaders of the North's society, economy, and politics. They owned the important industries and businesses. They held most public offices.

These Protestant values contributed to the growth of the Northern economy. They shaped Northern **capitalism**. Capitalism is an economic system that is based on private ownership of property and **free enterprise**.

Northern Protestants also believed strongly in social reform. For example, many avoided alcoholic drinks and formed **temperance**, or anti-alcohol, societies. Others helped create the first public schools and educational systems. Still others dedicated themselves to destroying what they saw as the greatest evil of their time: slavery. These people were called abolitionists.

This picture was used as the seal for the Society for the Abolition of Slavery in England in the 1780s. Poet John Greenleaf Whittier published it in the U.S. with his poem "Our Countrymen in Chains" in 1837. A quote with the image reads, "England has 800,000 slaves and she has made them free. America has 2,250,000! and she holds them fast!!!"

A Nation Divided: Causes of the Civil War

What Do You Know!

KNOW-NOTHING PARTY
In the 1850s, an anti-immigrant, anti-Catholic party formed. It was called the Know-Nothing Party, because when members were asked questions about their party and its beliefs, they often replied, "I know nothing."

Politics in the North

Two political parties dominated the North. The Whig Party was the party of business for the middle class who believed in a strong federal government. The Democratic Party appealed to outsiders in Northern society. These included recent immigrants, some rural people, and those who had not succeeded in the new Northern economy.

An important belief in the North was free labor. By the 1850s, many Northerners believed that people could begin with nothing and work their way up into the middle class or higher. Belief in the idea of free labor also influenced Northerners in another important way. It led many to see slavery as a terrible threat. Free laborers could lose their jobs if slaves became available to do those jobs.

How the North Saw the South

Many Northerners considered the South a roadblock to their continued economic progress. In the view of many Northerners, Southerners were lazy and cruel. They had slaves to do the hard work and profited from their misery. People in the North also resented the South's political power. Southern politicians were powerful enough to block many programs that Northerners wanted to put in place.

This sheet music cover entitled "The Know Nothing Quick Step" from 1854 pokes fun at the Know-Nothing Party. Men at the bottom of the sheet march holding a banner that displays a skull and crossbones.

> *I am not ashamed to confess that twenty five years ago I was a hired laborer... The free labor system opens the way for all—gives hope to all.*
>
> —Abraham Lincoln in 1860

Social and Cultural Divisions: North and South

The South

To most Southerners, the **census** of 1850 told an alarming tale. The North was growing 20 percent faster than the South. Seven of eight new immigrants chose to live in the North. The number of people moving from the South to the North was three times higher than the number moving from North to South. The South was also falling farther behind in industrial production, railroads, and canals. All this information strengthened the South's feelings of being left behind by the North. Dark clouds were gathering on the Southern economic horizon.

The Economy of the South

The only bright spot for the South was its agriculture. About 80 percent of Southern workers did agricultural work. The region's most important crop was cotton. Most cotton was grown on large farms known as **plantations**. The work of planting, growing, and harvesting the cotton was done by enslaved African Americans. The slaves lived on the plantations.

U.S. Cotton Production, 1790-1860	
Year	Pounds
1790	1,567,000
1800	36,572,500
1810	88,819,000
1820	167,189,000
1830	356,726,000
1840	673,116,000
1850	1,066,925,500
1860	1,918,701,000

Source: www.slaveryinamerica.org

Nearly all Southern cotton was sold to industries in the North and in Great Britain. Factories wove it into cloth. Southern cotton was shipped on Northern ships and British ships from ports like New Orleans. In all, little of the money earned from cotton remained in Southern pockets. This situation led Southerners to complain that they were "economic slaves" of the North.

Most cotton was grown in a region that spanned the deep South called the Cotton Belt. It stretched from South Carolina to Texas. The South grew other important crops as well. Tobacco was grown in Virginia and Kentucky. Rice thrived along the Atlantic coast, and sugar grew well in Louisiana. All these crops were grown using slave labor.

Southern Society

At the beginning of the Civil War, the population of the slaveholding states was about 12 million. In contrast, the North had about 22 million people. About one-third of Southerners were African-American slaves.

A Nation Divided: Causes of the Civil War

> "We want no manufactures; we desire no trading, no mechanical or manufacturing classes. As long as we have our rice, our sugar, our tobacco and our cotton, we can command wealth to purchase all we want."
>
> —Southern politician

Southern cotton was transported by steamship to ports such as New Orleans, then put on ocean-going ships for transport to Northern cities and Britain.

Most white Southerners did not own slaves. Only about 4 percent owned 20 or more slaves. Almost half of all whites owned no slaves at all. These Southerners were small farmers who owned their land, tenant farmers who rented land, or poor people. Very few Southerners worked in factories.

Even whites who did not own slaves supported slavery. Almost all Southerners believed that slavery was the key to their way of life. They feared the economic and social disaster that freeing the slaves would bring.

Social and Cultural Divisions: North and South

Owners of large plantations were the political leaders in the South. They led a life of privilege. This picture shows a plantation in Mississippi in the early 1800s.

The owners of the largest plantations were the political leaders of the South. They passed laws that benefited their class. They also helped spread an idea that gave stability to Southern society. No matter how poor a white man was, he was always better off than slaves. Poor whites who did not own slaves benefited because there was always someone below them on the social ladder. Although no schools taught this idea, Southerners understood how their society and economy was structured.

It is estimated that the 1 percent of slaveholders who held more than 20 slaves owned 20 percent to 30 percent of enslaved persons.

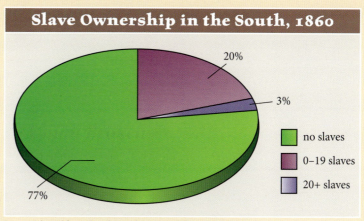

Slave Ownership in the South, 1860

- 77% no slaves
- 20% 0–19 slaves
- 3% 20+ slaves

Source: Adapted from *The Library of Congress Civil War Desk Reference*

Religion in the South

Like Americans in the North, most Southerners were Protestants. Louisiana had many Catholics because of its French history. Southern Protestantism was different from the Northern kind. To many in the South, religion was personal and focused on an individual's **salvation**. Southern Protestants cared less for social reform than did Northern Protestants. Although some Southerners wanted to abolish slavery, they were a tiny **minority**.

The South also lagged behind the North in education. Only one-third of white children were in school for three months a year. In New England, the figure was three-quarters.

The South did have temperance societies. Some plantation owners feared that the use of alcohol reduced the productivity of their slaves.

How the South Saw the North

Many Southerners considered Northerners to be unfeeling and greedy for money. Southern leaders often complained that Northerners were trying to destroy the South's economy, culture, and way of life by ending slavery.

Divided on Slavery

For almost four centuries, Europeans made more than 54,000 voyages trading slaves. At least 10 to 12 million Africans were forced to come to the Americas.

Slaves in the United States

The first slaves arrived in England's Jamestown colony in 1619. In less than a hundred years, England had become the world's largest slave-trading nation. Slaves lived in all the English colonies, not just colonies in the South. England banned its citizens from trading in enslaved people in 1807 and outlawed slavery completely in 1833.

The first Africans were brought to the Americas in the mid-1400s. Congress outlawed the slave trade in 1808. This meant that new enslaved people could not be brought to the United States. Slaves and their families already in the United States remained enslaved. By 1830, there were about two million slaves in the United States, most living in the South. Most slaves worked on farms with fewer than 20 slaves. They did skilled and unskilled jobs. Some worked in houses or craft shops. Few could read or write. Sometimes, families were split apart and sold to different owners. In spite of their difficult lives, slaves formed strong communities.

To many in the North, however, slavery went against every American value. In the years leading up to the Civil War, disagreements over slavery grew more and more fierce.

Major Events

1808
Atlantic slave trade outlawed

1831
Garrison's *The Liberator*, Nat Turner's rebellion

1850
Fugitive Slave Law

1852
Uncle Tom's Cabin published

1857
Dred Scott decision

1859
John Brown's raid

A Nation Divided: Causes of the Civil War

Slavery and Laws

By the end of the American Revolution, slavery had begun to die out in the North. An invention in 1793, however, made slaves even more important to the economy of the South. Eli Whitney's **cotton gin** (short for "engine") made it much easier to clean cotton. Cotton quickly replaced rice and tobacco as the South's main product. Cotton farming now required more slaves to keep up with production.

Limiting Slavery

By 1800, slavery had practically disappeared from the Northern states. Almost 200,000 free African Americans lived in the North by 1810. Most were not allowed to attend schools or vote, and many faced **discrimination**. Some became successful in various fields, owning land or running their own businesses, but most worked at unskilled, low-paying jobs. In major cities, free blacks formed community organizations and churches to support each other.

In 1808, the United States Congress took an important step. It outlawed the international slave trade. This meant that slaveholders could not bring in more slaves from Africa but the slave trade already within the United States continued. So they began to encourage their

---

People Before the War

John Newton

"Amazing Grace" is one of the best known of all Christian hymns. It tells the true story of the religious conversion of an English slave ship captain named John Newton. Newton wrote the poem in 1772 after accepting religion and rejecting his work as a slave trader.

This print condemns The Fugitive Slave Act of 1850. The law gave federal officials new powers to issue warrants for runaway slaves. The print shows armed officials firing rifles at four African Americans. One of the quotes at the bottom is from the Declaration of Independence: "We hold that all men are created equal…"

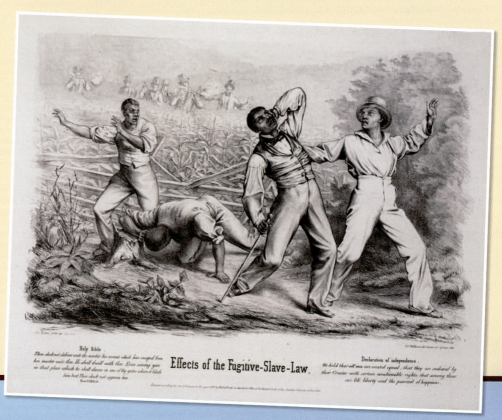

Divided on Slavery

slaves to have more children who would grow up to be slaves. Many owners also began treating their slaves better to ensure they would survive and have families.

Protecting Private Property

Laws also existed to protect the property of slaveholders. The Constitution guaranteed the right to take back any "person held to service or labor" who had escaped. Congress strengthened this right in 1793. It passed the first **fugitive slave law**. It stated that owners could cross state lines to recapture their runaways. Strangely, neither the Constitution nor the 1793 law used the word "slave."

In 1850, another fugitive slave law was passed. Southerners believed these laws protected their right to own people as property. Northerners considered slave catchers to be kidnappers.

In response to both laws, Northern states passed their own laws to protect fugitives. Northerners who wanted to help escaped slaves started the **Underground Railroad**. This was a series of safe houses where runaway slaves could hide until they could escape to Canada or other safe places.

Fugitive slave laws made people very angry on both sides. In 1854, a fugitive slave named Anthony Burns was captured in Boston. Thousands of Bostonians gathered to protest his return to slavery. One man was killed in an unsuccessful rescue attempt. Burns was returned to his owner by federal troops, but the event strengthened Northern resistance to the fugitive slave law. It also made the South more determined to protect its own rights and property.

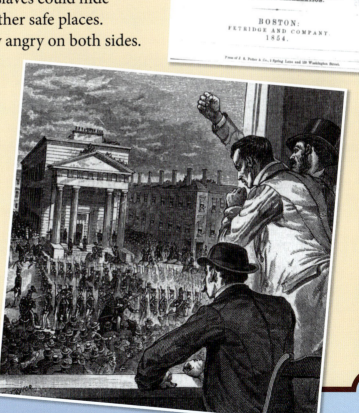

Title page from the book *Boston Slave Riot and Trial of Anthony Burns*, 1854

Boston citizens protesting an 1854 court order to return Anthony Burns to slavery in Virginia

A Nation Divided: Causes of the Civil War

Slavery and Popular Culture

Many Northern people in the 1800s had never seen a slave. Their ideas about slavery were shaped by **media** of the time. Books, newspapers, songs, and illustrations played an important role in how people, especially in the North, thought about slavery.

> *I do not wish to think, or speak, or write, with moderation—I will not retreat a single inch—AND I WILL BE HEARD.*
>
> —William Lloyd Garrison in *The Liberator*, 1831

Abolitionist Newspapers

In 1831, a Massachusetts writer named William Lloyd Garrison started an abolitionist newspaper, *The Liberator*. For 30 years, he was a tireless supporter of immediate **emancipation,** or freeing, of all slaves. He publicly burned a copy of the Constitution on July 4th to protest the 1850 fugitive slave law. *The Liberator* influenced many Northerners' views of slavery.

Harriet Beecher Stowe

Uncle Tom's Cabin

Harriet Beecher Stowe created the most powerful media image of slavery in 1852. Stowe wrote her novel *Uncle Tom's Cabin* in response to the recent fugitive slave law. It was the fictional story about a slave family's suffering and attempts to escape slavery. Stowe based her book on a slave auction she witnessed in Kentucky as a girl, stories she was told by escaped slaves she met while living in Cincinnati, Ohio, and contemporary interviews in magazines and newspapers. It was the best-selling novel of the time, selling 300,000 copies in its first year of publication.

Eva and Topsy, two characters from Harriet Beecher Stowe's *Uncle Tom's Cabin*

The book was hugely influential in both the North and South. Even President Abraham Lincoln gave credit to the book. When he met Stowe in 1862, he reportedly said, "So you're the little woman who started this great war." The story enraged Southerners. Many pro-slavery responses were written. They claimed that slaves were not mistreated and, in fact, had better lives than Northern workers.

Rising Tensions Over Slavery

From 1800 to 1860, tensions over slavery heated up. Several events over this period became stepping-stones to the outbreak of war. One of these was the Missouri Compromise of 1820. This agreement tried to cool tempers over the spread of slavery to new states in the Union, but it was not a long-term solution.

As the years passed, attitudes became more extreme. Everyone wondered how the disagreement over slavery would be solved. Some feared the worst could not be avoided.

Slave Rebellions

Many Southerners feared that enslaved people would arm themselves and rebel against their captivity. The successful revolution on the Caribbean island of Haiti in 1804 inspired many slaves in the South. Some took up arms against their masters. All ended in brutal defeats for the slaves, but each rebellion made whites more fearful.

This cartoon shows a Southern view of slavery in response to abolition. It depicts "slavery as it exists in America" (top) as happy slaves singing and dancing. The lower panel, "slavery as it exists in England," shows downtrodden factory workers.

A Nation Divided: Causes of the Civil War

A deeply religious Virginia slave named Nat Turner believed he saw signs and heard voices from heaven. Turner felt they were telling him to take up arms against the slaveholders. In summer 1831, an eclipse of the sun told him the time had come. With about 40 followers, Turner went on a killing spree. Before he was captured and executed, his band had killed more than 50 white people.

Turner's rebellion terrified whites throughout the South. The Virginia legislature decided to create new, much harsher laws for dealing with slaves.

The Supreme Court Speaks

The next event that raised tensions between North and South occurred in 1857. Dred Scott was an enslaved man that lived in Louisiana and Missouri. His owner had taken him to Illinois, where slavery was banned. Later they moved back to Missouri, where slavery was legal. After his master died, Scott tried to buy the freedom of himself and his family but was refused. Scott filed a lawsuit claiming that he should be free because he had lived in a free state. Scott's case went all the way to the U.S. Supreme Court.

Americans watched the case closely. It would set the law for future cases. Of the nine justices, five were Southerners. Two more were Northern Democrats. Americans in the North and South wondered how the Court would rule.

Americans got their answer when Dred Scott lost his case. The Dred Scott decision made three important points:
1. African Americans were not citizens and had no rights.
2. Slaves were nothing more than property.
3. Congress had no right to ban slavery anywhere.

Dred Scott and his family, 1857

> *A house divided against itself cannot stand. I believe this government cannot endure, permanently half slave and half free.*
>
> —Senate candidate Abraham Lincoln, in 1858, on the Dred Scott decision

Divided on Slavery

Northerners were stunned. The pro-slavery Supreme Court had overturned laws made by the anti-slavery majority. Even Northerners who were not opposed to slavery were concerned. Many of them began to change their minds. Southerners rejoiced because they believed the anti-slavery forces had been defeated for good.

"This Guilty Land"

By the end of the 1850s, Northern abolitionists were desperate. Slavery was spreading, slowly but surely, and it seemed there was no way to stop it. One man named John Brown thought he knew a way.

John Brown was an unsuccessful farmer and businessman from Connecticut. He was deeply religious and inspired by the prophets of the Bible's Old Testament. He had traveled to Kansas in 1855 to help slavery opponents battle slavery supporters. Over the next few years, Brown secretly planned a shocking campaign. On October 16, 1859, he set his plan in action.

Brown and 21 followers attacked the federal **arsenal**, or weapons storehouse, in Harper's Ferry, Virginia. He planned to steal weapons. He would give them to the runaway slaves he expected to join his cause. Together they would wage war against slaveholders. His plan failed and Brown was quickly captured by federal soldiers.

U.S. Marines storm the engine house occupied by John Brown and his men at Harper's Ferry, Virginia, October 18, 1859

A Nation Divided: Causes of the Civil War

Brown was convicted and hanged. He wrote a letter before his execution. His prediction proved accurate: "I . . . am now quite certain that the crimes of this guilty land will never be purged away but with Blood."

Reactions to Brown

Southerners were horrified by John Brown's raid. They saw it as final proof that the North would not stop until it had destroyed the South's way of life.

At first, most Northerners disapproved as well. They felt Brown's bloody solution to the problem of slavery was too extreme. Many Northerners even supported slavery and considered African Americans inferior to whites. Public opinion began to change, though. Brown's quiet dignity at his trial impressed many. Soon, some Northerners began to speak of him as a hero and **martyr**. Only he had been brave enough to strike back at the slaveholders.

As the North's opinion of Brown's raid changed, Southerners became even angrier. There were stories of unexplained fires started by slaves throughout the South. Were slavery opponents following John Brown's bloody example? No one knew for sure. But many Southerners were ready to fight fire with fire.

As John Brown is led to the gallows, he stops to kiss an African-American baby held by its mother. John Brown became an inspiration for the cause of abolition.

Political Divisions

President George Washington retired from politics in 1796. In his Farewell Address, he warned Americans about the dangers of political parties. A country that had once been united in fighting for freedom from British rule was beginning to divide into smaller groups. He was alarmed at the negative effects of political divisions on Americans. Yet even in his own administration, the seeds of party politics had been planted.

Political Parties Disagree About Slavery

The Constitution said nothing about political parties. People realized quickly that political parties were a way to communicate their ideas and influence the government, though. Parties expressed ideas and voters supported candidates based on these ideas. By the 1830s, parties were firmly established. Their ideas changed in response to the issues of the time.

Beginning in the 1830s, the Democrats and the Whigs were the major political parties. In the early 1850s, the Whig Party dissolved through disagreement over the issue of expanding slavery into new states. Americans wondered what party would take its place.

Major Events

1840 Liberty Party formed

1846–47 War with Mexico

1848 Free Soil Party nominates presidential candidate

1850 Compromise of 1850

1854 Kansas-Nebraska Act, Republican Party formed

1857 Dred Scott decision

A Nation Divided: Causes of the Civil War

National Political Parties

The first political parties were national. Some were stronger in certain areas of the country than others. Regional preferences for one party over another became apparent.

The Democratic Party

The Democratic Party was based on the ideas of Thomas Jefferson, James Madison, and Andrew Jackson. Democrats were generally concerned with the interests of farmers and other common people, including immigrants and laborers. They opposed wealthy businessmen, bankers, and factory owners who they thought became rich at the expense of poorer people. They were suspicious of a powerful federal government. Instead, they supported **states' rights**. This is the idea that the power of the individual states should be greater than the power of the federal government. Supporters of states' rights believed that laws made by a state should overrule laws made by the federal government.

By 1860, Democrats had split into two groups. Most Northern Democrats supported **popular sovereignty**. This idea said that states could decide for themselves if they would have slavery or not. Other Northern Democrats opposed the spread of slavery. Southern Democrats supported slavery. This split in the party proved fatal in the presidential election of 1860.

The Republican Party

The Republican Party was formed in 1854, mainly to oppose slavery and its spread to new territories. It was made up of anti-slavery Whigs, Northern Democrats, abolitionists, and members of other smaller parties. The new party nominated its first presidential candidate, John C. Frémont. In the election of 1856, Frémont lost to Democrat James Buchanan but, over the next four years, events helped the party gain many supporters.

Other Parties

Several smaller parties also shared the political landscape of the 1840s and 1850s. The first party formed to battle slavery was the Liberty Party. It was created in 1839. Southerners worried about a party dedicated to destroying slavery.

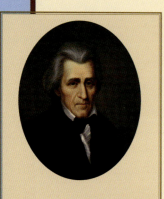

People Before the War
Andrew Jackson

Americans had strong feelings about President Andrew Jackson. A hero of the War of 1812, he was elected president in 1828. To his supporters, he was the first common man to enter the White House. But to his enemies, he was rough, hotheaded, and uneducated. His presidency was filled with bitter political fights. Jackson created the modern political party by giving jobs to his supporters. He was such an important figure that all his opponents banded together to form the Whig Party. His supporters became the Democratic Party.

Political Divisions

A larger, more successful party appeared in 1848. This was the Free Soil Party. This party wanted to prevent slavery from spreading into newly acquired territories. It wanted to keep this land for free white Northerners.

The rise of new parties had an important effect. From then on, candidates would have to offer solutions to the problem of slavery. They could no longer try to ignore it.

Martin Van Buren was the presidential candidate of the Free Soil Party in 1848. The party opposed the expansion of slavery, but did not support abolition. The party got only 10 percent of the popular vote due to lack of support from abolitionists. The cartoon shows Van Buren unsuccessfully trying to bridge the gap between the Democratic platform and the Whig-Abolition platform.

Western Expansion Raises Tensions

As the country spread westward, the ghost of slavery haunted the new territories. Americans asked themselves whether new territories should allow slavery or ban it. It was a question that would have many different answers.

In 1836, Americans living in the Mexican territory of Texas declared their independence from Mexico. The new Republic of Texas had a government and constitution similar to the U.S. government. Slavery was legal under the Texas Constitution, though. Texas remained independent until 1845, when it agreed to become part of the United States.

In 1846, the United States and Britain signed a treaty that divided the Oregon Country between the two, along Oregon's current northern border. It included what are now the states of Oregon, Washington, and Idaho, as well as parts of Montana and Wyoming. Oregon became an organized U.S. Territory in 1848. Slavery was not allowed under the Oregon Constitution.

War with Mexico

In 1846, the United States went to war with Mexico. The American victory a year later brought new territory. In the peace treaty, Mexico

A Nation Divided: Causes of the Civil War

gave up much of its land to the United States in what is now the American southwest. The United States gained more than 500,000 square miles (1.3 million km^2). Northerners feared that most of this new territory would become slave states.

To prevent that from happening, a Pennsylvania congressman named David Wilmot proposed that no territory gained from Mexico should allow slavery. Congress voted on his proposal, called the Wilmot Proviso. A **proviso** is a restriction. Northern Democrats and Whigs in the House voted together in favor of the Wilmot Proviso. The Senate also voted. With 15 slave states and 14 free states in Congress, senators from slave states voted against the Proviso so it did not become law. This was the first time that Congress had divided by section, not by party. It was a fateful change.

Congress Addresses Slavery

Changes in the nation's population also had an impact on the argument over slavery. A state's population determines the number of representatives from that state in the House of Representatives. The number of free states was growing faster than the number of slave states. As a result, free states were gradually gaining more representation than slave states.

The Senate has two members from each state, regardless of population. In the Senate, Southerners were better able to preserve the balance between free and slave states. They were helped by some Northerners, called Doughfaces, who supported slavery.

The Compromise of 1850

The simmering battle over the balance of free states and slave states boiled over in 1849. California, whose population exploded when gold was discovered in 1848, was ready to become a state. California's two senators would tip the balance in the Senate toward free states. Two other areas, Utah and New Mexico, wanted to become territories. Would these territories allow or forbid slavery? Southerners opposed any addition that would tip the balance of

> *I wish to speak to you today, not as a Massachusetts man, nor as a Northern man, but as an American.*
> —Daniel Webster, speaking in support of the Compromise of 1850

Political Divisions

power against slavery. Some extremists began talking of **secession**, or leaving the Union.

Henry Clay, a main author of the Missouri Compromise 30 years earlier, had a plan. He proposed a series of bills that became known as the Compromise of 1850. After much bitter debate, Congress agreed on several important ideas.

California would join the union as a free state. Utah and New Mexico would become territories with popular sovereignty. Their citizens would decide for themselves about slavery. The slave trade would be outlawed in the District of Columbia. A stronger fugitive slave law would be passed.

Pro-slavery and anti-slavery **radicals** were angered by the agreements. Most Americans were satisfied, though. They hoped the compromise had finally solved the slavery problem for good.

The Kansas-Nebraska Act

The two-party system of Whigs and Democrats was finally destroyed in 1854. Kansas and Nebraska were ready to become territories. The Missouri Compromise of 1820 banned slavery north of the latitude line 36°30′N. This meant that the new territories of Kansas and Nebraska would be free states. Southerners would not, however, approve two new free states. A Democratic senator from Illinois, Stephen A. Douglas, proposed canceling the Missouri Compromise.

> **What Do You Know?**
>
> **LINCOLN-DOUGLAS DEBATES**
>
> At five feet four inches tall, Stephen A. Douglas was known as the Little Giant. In 1858, his Republican opponent in the Senate election was a tall, lanky, lawyer named Abraham Lincoln. During the campaign, they had a series of debates considered the greatest in U.S. history. Douglas won the election. The two would face off for the presidency two years later, with a very different outcome.

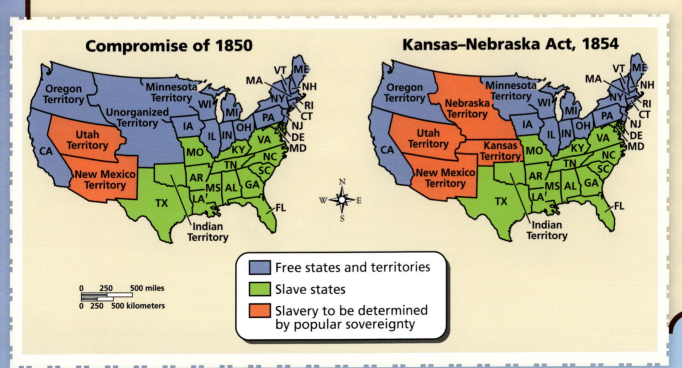

A Nation Divided: Causes of the Civil War

The residents of each state would then decide to become free or slave states. Together, Douglas and President Franklin Pierce convinced enough senators and congressmen to back the proposal.

Passing the Kansas–Nebraska Act had several effects. Douglas became famous and a leading candidate for the Democratic presidential nomination. Kansas became a bloody battleground. Slavery supporters and opponents, including John Brown, flocked to the state to try to influence its future. It earned the name "Bleeding Kansas." Abolitionists quickly realized they would need a new political party dedicated to ending slavery.

Blood Flows in the Senate

Abolitionists' hopes would soon be crushed. As the 1850s passed, anger rose and tempers flared. In 1856, pro-slavery and anti-slavery forces battled viciously in the disputed territory of Kansas. Politicians in Washington supported one side or the other. Anti-slavery leader Charles Sumner of Massachusetts gave an angry speech in the Senate. He harshly condemned slavery and insulted Southern leaders.

The speech so enraged South Carolina Congressman Preston Brooks that he approached Sumner in the Senate. He beat him with a heavy cane. Sumner collapsed, covered in blood. He never completely recovered. Southerners praised the beating. They felt it defended the honor of the South. Northerners were shocked. They saw it as another example of the South's brutality. Some even compared Sumner's beating to the whipping of slaves.

Preston Brooks beating Charles Sumner in the U.S. Congress, May 22, 1856

The Election of 1860

The nation was tense and even more divided leading up to the election year of 1860. John Brown had just been hanged. Tempers remained at a fever pitch. Southern men joined **militias**. Southern legislatures began buying arms.

The Nominating Conventions

The national political parties all had serious weaknesses caused by decades of compromises over slavery. No party had support in all parts of the country. The Whigs were gone. The Democrats were hopelessly divided by sectionalism and opinions about slavery. The Republicans, while strong in the North, had no support in the South. Even the Methodist and Baptist churches split into Northern anti-slavery and Southern pro-slavery groups.

American political parties gathered in the spring to nominate candidates and write **platforms**, or statements of party beliefs. As the parties gathered at nominating conventions, Americans feared what might happen.

Democrats: Fire-eaters and Walkouts

Democrats met for their convention in Charleston, South Carolina. Delegates from the North felt as though they were in enemy territory. Some extreme Southern Democrats known as **fire-eaters** were already threatening to walk out. They demanded that the convention approve a

Major Events

1859

December
John Brown hanged

1860

April
Democrats in Charleston fail to nominate a candidate

May
Constitutional Unionists nominate Bell
Republicans nominate Lincoln

June
Northern Democrats nominate Douglas
Southern Democrats nominate Breckinridge

November
Lincoln wins election with 40 percent of the popular vote

A Nation Divided: Causes of the Civil War

Stephen A. Douglas

platform that protected slavery. Northerners, led by Stephen A. Douglas, viewed such an action as political suicide for them. The Democrats needed to find a way to unite for the fall election.

The leading fire-eater, William Yancey, led a walkout when the convention approved a platform upholding popular sovereignty. Disappointed delegates went home without a nominee. They decided to meet again in Baltimore, Maryland, six weeks later.

The second convention ended in another walkout by slavery supporters. Southerners met quickly and nominated Vice-President John C. Breckinridge. They adopted a pro-slavery platform. Many Democrats knew their divided party had little chance against a united Republican Party.

Honest Abe at the Wigwam

Republicans met at a huge building called the Wigwam in Chicago, Illinois. The leading candidates were anti-slavery crusader William Seward from New York and Abraham Lincoln from Illinois. Lincoln had become known for his debates with Stephen A. Douglas in 1858. Delegates considered Seward too radical to win the election and chose Lincoln. Lincoln's reputation for honesty earned him the nickname "Honest Abe."

John C. Breckinridge

The Republican platform was cleverly written. While it did not change any of the party's anti-slavery ideas, it made them more acceptable to voters in the middle. The platform condemned John Brown's raid, but it also warned Southerners about **treason**.

The fourth candidate, John C. Bell, headed the Constitutional Unionist Party ticket. The party, composed of former Whigs, tried to ignore the slavery issue and promised to uphold the Constitution.

The Campaign of 1860

Abraham Lincoln, May 20, 1860

The campaign was really two elections. In the North, it was Lincoln against Douglas. Republican Lincoln was not even listed on the ballot in some Southern states. In the South, the race was between Breckinridge and Bell. Douglas claimed he was the only *national* candidate. He received little support in the South.

The Election of 1860

Charges Fly

Northern Democrats argued that if Lincoln were elected it would certainly destroy the Union. They charged that Lincoln would encourage freed African Americans to take jobs from white workers. Republicans accused the Democrats, under President James Buchanan's administration, of corruption and the financial abuse of power. Republicans also claimed Douglas would not oppose the spread of slavery.

The Nation Watches and Worries

Meanwhile, Southerners waited. Most people felt Lincoln would be elected. This pleased the fire-eaters. This would make Southerners flock to the banner of secession. Others were sad at the likely breakup of the Union.

As the election approached, hysteria increased in the South. Rumors spread about slaves setting fires after encouragement from mysterious Northern visitors. Secession rallies drew huge crowds in Southern cities. In the North, many felt the South was trying to scare the North by saying, "Elect a Democrat, or you will destroy the Union."

This cartoon of the election of 1860 shows rival candidates for president, Abraham Lincoln (top) and Stephen A. Douglas, in a footrace toward the U.S. Capitol. Lincoln, with his huge stride, has the advantage. Douglas wonders how he will get over the fence. Just over the fence is a slave, a reference to the issue of slavery in the election.

Counting the Votes

Lincoln was carried to victory on a sea of Northern votes. Anti-slavery Republicans also strengthened Republican control of Congress. Lincoln carried every Northern state, along with Oregon and California. He won 40 percent of the popular vote and 180 of 303 electoral votes. He received no support in the South. Douglas won Missouri only, but he finished second in the popular vote with 29 percent. Breckinridge won all the Southern states, plus Delaware and Maryland. Bell took Tennessee, Kentucky, and Virginia.

Americans tried to understand the meaning of the election results. Each side considered the other to be fanatics, radicals, or devils. Many in the North would have agreed with Charles Francis Adams, the son and grandson of presidents, who said, "The great revolution has actually taken place. . . . The country has once and for all thrown off the

A Nation Divided: Causes of the Civil War

domination of the Slaveholders."

For Southerners, the writing was on the wall. The country would soon be governed by those who hated slavery. A New Orleans newspaper called every Northern vote for Lincoln, "a deliberate, cold-blooded insult and outrage to Southern honor."

> *I think I see in the future a gory head rise above our horizon. Its name is Civil War. Already I can see the prints of his bloody fingers upon our . . . doorposts*
> —Thomas Reade Rootes Cobb, Georgia secession leader, 1860

Even though Lincoln would not become president until March 1861, the wheels of secession were already turning. President Buchanan, a Doughface Democrat, tried desperately to keep the Southern states in the Union. But the time for compromises was over.

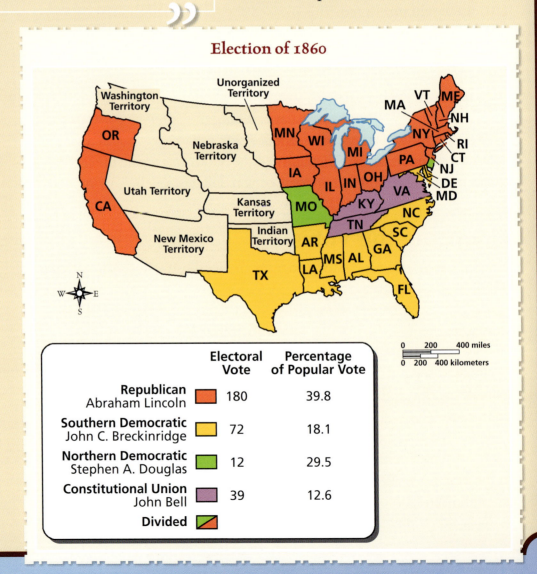

Election of 1860

Candidate	Electoral Vote	Percentage of Popular Vote
Republican — Abraham Lincoln	180	39.8
Southern Democratic — John C. Breckinridge	72	18.1
Northern Democratic — Stephen A. Douglas	12	29.5
Constitutional Union — John Bell	39	12.6
Divided		

The Union Broken

Southern states moved quickly. Following Lincoln's victory, while Buchanan was still president, several states decided to leave the Union. The first was South Carolina, home of the most radical fire-eating secessionists. Six other states swiftly followed. In all but one state, Texas, the decision was made by state legislatures, not by voters. About 80 percent of Texas voters approved secession.

Southerners hoped that their secession from the Union would be peaceful, but began organizing an army in case it was not. Their goal was to assemble 100,000 soldiers in case they were needed. At the beginning of 1861, the United States had only about 16,000 soldiers in its army.

Major Events

1860
December
South Carolina secedes, followed by six other states

1861
February
Confederate States of America formed in Montgomery, Alabama

1861
March
Lincoln takes office

1861
April
Civil War begins

> *You people of the South don't know what you are doing. This country will be drenched in blood, and God only knows how it will end. It is all folly, madness, a crime against civilization.*
>
> —William T. Sherman (later one of the North's greatest generals)

A Nation Divided: Causes of the Civil War

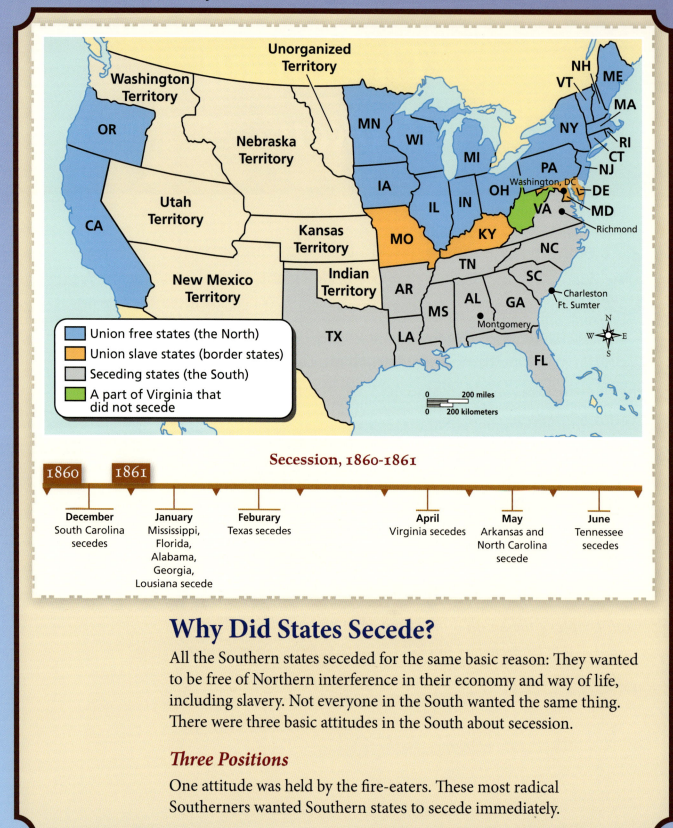

Secession, 1860-1861

Why Did States Secede?

All the Southern states seceded for the same basic reason: They wanted to be free of Northern interference in their economy and way of life, including slavery. Not everyone in the South wanted the same thing. There were three basic attitudes in the South about secession.

Three Positions

One attitude was held by the fire-eaters. These most radical Southerners wanted Southern states to secede immediately.

The Union Broken

After several states had seceded, they would meet to organize a new country and its government. This group was the largest.

Another smaller group, called Cooperationists, wanted Southern states to meet and organize before seceding. They believed a united South would be stronger. It would have a better chance of working together and surviving as a new country.

> "To secede from the Union and set up another government would cause war. . . . It [war] will take the flower of the country—the young men."
> —Sam Houston, to his fellow Texans

A small group of Southerners were opposed to secession. They had different reasons. Some feared secession and civil war would destroy slavery and the South. Among them was Sam Houston, the founder and governor of Texas, who was forced from office. Some were against immediate secession. They felt Lincoln should be given a chance to compromise with the South.

This print ridicules the secession movement in 1861. South Carolina is in the lead headed toward a cliff, shown by a man riding a pig. Florida, Alabama, Mississippi, and Louisiana follow, represented by men on mules. The man representing Georgia rides down the hill and confesses, "We have some doubts about the end of the road. . . ."

A Nation Divided: Causes of the Civil War

> *Secession is not intended to break up the present government. . . . We do not propose breaking up or destroying the Union as our fathers gave it to us, but we go out for the purpose of getting . . . security for our rights.*
>
> —A.H. Handy of Mississippi, 1860, explaining secession in Baltimore

Reading the Constitution

Was secession legal? Not surprisingly, the North and South had different opinions. The Constitution said nothing about states leaving the Union after they have joined.

Most Southerners believed secession was legal. They believed that state government should have more power and rights than the federal government. If the states created the nation, they reasoned, then the states could take it apart.

Other Southerners believed in the "right of revolution." They argued that people had the right to rebel against an unjust government—just as the American colonies did in 1776. Seceding was the only way Southerners could protect their freedom, including the freedom to own slaves. They accused Northerners of being revolutionaries, determined to destroy the South's way of life.

Emancipation or Not?

Northerners thought the Southern position was ridiculous. They didn't understand how anybody's idea of freedom could include holding other human beings in slavery. Many Northerners wanted to free all the slaves in the South. Others were not in favor of emancipation. In addition, Northerners did not believe states had a right to secede. The nation came before the individual states.

> *If we do not make common cause to save the good old ship of the Union on this voyage, nobody will have a chance to pilot her on another voyage.*
>
> —Abraham Lincoln, February 1861

The Road to War

In February 1861, the seven states that had seceded met in Montgomery, Alabama. There, they created a new nation and wrote a constitution, which protected slavery. Jefferson Davis of Mississippi was elected as president of the Confederate States of America during a convention held in Alabama in 1861. The first business of the new nation was to convince other slave states to secede from the United States and join them.

Meanwhile in Washington, outgoing President Buchanan refused to recognize secession and the new nation. He announced that the government would continue to collect taxes in the Southern states. He kept federal forts open. He also blamed the North for treating the South unfairly. He demanded that the North make many concessions to keep the South in the Union. Republicans, who had just won the election, howled in anger. They considered Buchanan's demands a surrender to the South.

Jefferson Davis, president of the Confederacy

> *... Senators, we recur [return] to the compact which binds us together; we recur to the principles on which our government was founded; and when you deny them, and when you deny to us the right to withdraw from a government which ... threatens to be destructive of our rights, we but tread in the path of our fathers when we proclaim our independence, and take the hazard.*
>
> —Jefferson Davis to the U.S. Senate, January 21, 1861

A Nation Divided: Causes of the Civil War

Did Slavery Cause the Civil War?

Both North and South claimed to be defending the Constitution. Southerners argued that their self-government and liberty were protected by the Constitution. Northerners replied that the Union could not be broken by individual states. At the start of the war, neither side admitted it was fighting over slavery. In the North, waging an anti-slavery war would have threatened unity—many Northerners were not for emancipation. This would change by the end of the war. Southerners spoke of defending their way of life and did not mention slavery. Most people, however, knew that slavery was a key part of the Southern way of life. Even Southerners who did not own slaves fought to protect the rights of those who did.

Echoes Today

While secession and slavery are gone, many of the issues that led to the Civil War are still important today. The proper roles of the federal government and the states are still debated. People question how much power the federal government should have. The problem of racism raises the question of whether the descendents of slaves and slave owners are fully equal in today's America. How Americans should solve political disagreements is a daily topic in the news. Disagreements between the federal government and individual states have cropped up on topics as varied as health care, global warming, and creating jobs. The issues that rose up in 1861 are still a presence today.

> *We hold as undeniable truths that the government of the various states . . . were established exclusively by the white race . . . that the African race had no agency [part] in their establishment; that they were rightfully held and regarded as an inferior and dependent race, and in that condition only could their existence in this country be rendered beneficial or tolerable.*
>
> —"A Declaration of Causes Which Impel the State of Texas to Secede from the Union," February 2, 1861

GLOSSARY

abolitionist A person who argued for the end of slavery in the United States
arsenal A place where military arms and ammunition are stored

capitalism An economic system in which businesses and wealth are owned and managed by individuals rather than by the government
census A count of the population
compromise A settlement of issues among people or groups with opposing ideas or demands
cotton gin An invention that separates seeds from cotton fibers

discrimination To distinguish among people or things; to show favor for or against, sometimes unfairly
domination The situation of being controlled or ruled over by others

emancipation Being freed from enslavement
endorse To state one's support or approval of an idea or individual

federal The central government of a union of states
fire-eaters Southern political leaders who argued that pro-slavery states should separate from the Union to form the Confederate States of America

free enterprise A competitive, free-market economic system in which individuals invest their money in a business to make a profit
fugitive slave law Law passed in 1850 requiring that runaway slaves be returned to their masters

industrial output A measure of the goods produced by industry
industry Manufacturers of products

martyr A person who suffers greatly for a belief or cause
media A method of communicating to a wide audience, for example, through books or newspapers
militia A unit of citizen soldiers within a state, often called upon during emergencies
minority a group or political party that is smaller than the majority or greater part

nullify To legally declare that a law is void or invalid

plantation A large farm worked by a group of slaves or laborers that produces crops for market
platform A statement of the beliefs of a political party
popular sovereignty The freedom of people in U.S. territories or states to determine by vote whether to accept or reject slavery

Glossary

proviso A clause in a law or contract stating a condition or restriction

radicals People who take an extreme position on an issue

rural Areas outside the city that are considered to be the country

salvation Being saved from sin

secession The withdrawal of Southern states from the United States to set up a separate nation called the Confederate States of America

sectional crisis Crisis brought about by divisiveness among different regions of a nation

sectionalism A focus on local or regional concerns over the concerns of a nation

standard of living The level of economic comfort that a person, family, or community has in everyday life

states' rights The right of states to make their own laws and manage their own affairs without interference from the federal government

temperance Moderation; for example, observing limits on the consumption of alcohol

treason A betrayal of one's country

Underground Railroad A network of people who helped slaves escape to free states or Canada before and during the Civil War

urban Relating to the city

MORE INFORMATION

Books

Bolotin, Norman. *Civil War A to Z: A Young Person's Guide to Over 100 People, Places, and Points of Importance.* Dutton Children's Books, 2002.

De Saussure, N. B. *Old Plantation Days; Being Recollections of Southern Life Before the Civil War.* The Trow Press, 1909.

Elliot, Henry. *Frederick Douglass: From Slavery to Statesman.* Crabtree Publishing Company, 2010.

Foner, Eric. *Free Soil, Free Labor, Free Men: The Ideology of the Republican Party before the Civil War.* Oxford University Press, 1995.

Goodheart, Adam. *1861: The Civil War Awakening.* New York: Alfred A. Knopf, 2011.

Harrold, Stanley. *Border War: Fighting over Slavery before the Civil War.* The University of North Carolina Press, 2010.

Herbert, Janis. *The Civil War for Kids: A History with 21 Activities* (For Kids series) Chicago Review Press, 1999.

Horn, Geoffrey M. *John Brown: Putting Actions Above Words.* Crabtree Publishing Company, 2010.

McPherson, James M. *The Illustrated Battle Cry of Freedom: The Civil War Era.* Oxford University Press, 2003.

Websites

http://www.archives.gov/research/african-americans/
African-American heritage page of the National Archives website. Contains records for genealogists and social historians and information about the history of the Freedmen's Bureau.

http://memory.loc.gov/ammem/aaohtml/exhibit/aopart1.html
Library of Congress site on the institution of slavery and slavery rebellions. Includes artwork, photos, and facts.

http://memory.loc.gov/ammem/aaohtml/exhibit/aopart3.html
Library of Congress site on abolition and the rise of sectionalism before the Civil War. Includes artwork, photos, and facts.

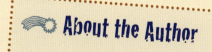

About the Author

Jeff Putnam is a freelance educational writer from Mount Vernon, Ohio.

INDEX

abolitionists, 10, 15, 24, 27, 30, 31, 34
African Americans, 6, 10, 17, 22, 26, 28, 37
American Anti-Slavery Society, 5

Bell, John C., 5, 35–38
Bleeding Kansas, 34
border states, 14, 40
Breckinridge, John C., 5, 35–38
Brooks, Preston, 34
Brown, John, 21, 27, 28, 34–36
Buchanan, James, 30, 36-39, 43
Burns, Anthony, 23

canals, 6, 8, 14, 17
capitalism, 15
census, 17
Clay, Henry, 13, 33
Compromise of 1850, 29, 32, 33
Confederate States of America, 39, 43
Congress, U.S., 8, 12, 13, 21–23, 26, 32–34, 37
constitution
    Confederate, 42
    Oregon, 31
    Texas, 31
    U.S., 5, 6, 10, 12, 23, 24, 29, 36, 41, 42, 44
Constitutional Union Party, 5, 35, 36, 38
Cooperationists, 41
cotton gin, 12, 22
cotton production, 9, 12, 17
culture
    Northern, 14
    Southern, 20, 24

Davis, Jefferson, 43
Democratic Party, 5, 16, 29, 30–33, 38
Democrats
    Northern, 5, 26, 30, 35, 38
    Southern, 5, 30, 35, 38
discrimination, 21, 22
Dixon, Jeremiah, 11, 12
Doughface Democrat, 32, 38
Douglas, Stephen A., 5, 33–38
Dred Scott decision, 21, 26, 29

economy
    of the North, 14–16
    of the South, 17, 19, 20, 22, 40
election of 1856, 30
election of 1860, 5, 30, 35–38, 43

emancipation, 24, 42, 44
Erie Canal, 5

farming
    Southern, 9, 17, 18, 22
    Northern, 14
    See also plantations
federal government, 6, 16, 30, 42, 44
fire-eaters, 35–37, 39, 40
Free Soil Party, 29, 31
free states, 5, 13, 14, 32, 33, 40
Frémont, John C., 30
fugitive slave laws, 21–24, 33

Garrison, William L., 21, 24
Great Britain, 7, 13, 17

Harper's Ferry, 27
Houston, Sam, 41

immigrants, 7, 9, 14, 16, 17, 30
immigration, 7, 9, 14
industrial output, 8, 17
industries, 6, 9, 15, 17

Jackson, Andrew, 10, 30
Jefferson, Thomas, 8, 30

Kansas-Nebraska Act, 29, 33, 34
Know-Nothing Party, 16

Liberator, The, 21, 24
Liberty Party, 29, 30
Lincoln, Abraham, 5, 16, 17, 25, 26, 33, 35–39, 41, 42
Lincoln-Douglas debates, 33, 36
Louisiana
    Purchase, 5, 8, 9
    Territory, 8, 11, 12

Mason, Charles, 11, 12
Mason-Dixon Line, 11, 12
militias, 35
Mississippi River, 12
Missouri Compromise, 11–14, 25, 33
newspapers
    abolitionist, 24
    of New Orleans, 38

Newton, John, 22
Northwest Territory, 11, 12
nullification, 10

Pierce, Franklin, 34
plantations, 9, 17, 19
politics, Northern, 15, 16
popular sovereignty, 30, 33, 36
population, 6, 7, 14, 17, 32

railroads, 6, 8, 9, 14, 17
rebellion, slave, 21, 25, 26
religion, 9, 11, 14, 15, 20, 22
    Catholic, 15
    in the North, 15
    Protestant, 15
    in the South, 20
Republican Party, 5, 29, 30, 35–38, 43

salvation, 20
secession, 33, 37–43
    reasons for, 40–42
sectionalism, 9, 35
slave ownership in the South (chart), 19
slave states, 13, 32, 33, 40
slave trade, 5, 10, 21, 22, 33
slavery, 5, 6, 9, 10, 12–15, 17, 18, 20–38, 40–44
    as cause of Civil War, 44
    history of, 21
    and politics, 29–34, 35–38
    and racism, 28, 44
slaves, 9, 10, 12, 13, 15–18, 20–23, 25–27, 34, 37, 42, 44
society
    Northern, 15, 16
    Southern, 12, 17, 19
standard of living, 8
states' rights, 30
Sumner, Charles, 34
Supreme Court, U.S., 26, 27

temperance, 15, 20
Turner, Nat, 21, 26

Uncle Tom's Cabin, 21, 24
Underground Railroad, 23

Van Buren, Martin, 31

War of 1812, 8, 30
Washington, George
    Farewell Address, 29
Whig Party, 16, 29–33, 35, 36
Wilmot Proviso, 32